Collins
My First Book of
Transport

Collins My First Book of Transport
Collins
An imprint of HarperCollins Publishers
Westerhill Road
Bishopbriggs
Glasgow
G64 2QT

First edition 2011
Second edition 2013

Copyright © Q2AMEDIA 2011

ISBN 978-0-00-752118-0
ISBN 978-0-00-752321-4

Imp 001

Collins® is a registered trademark of

HarperCollins Publishers Limited
www.collinslanguage.com
A catalogue record for this book is available from the British Library

Printed by South China Printing Company, China

Author: Ian Graham
Editor: Jean Coppendale
Project Manager: Shekhar Kapur
Art Director: Joita Das
Designers: Ankita Sharma, Deepika Verma and Jasmeen Kaur
Picture Researchers: Akansha Srivastava and Saloni Vaid

For the Publisher:
Elaine Higgleton
Ruth O'Donovan

Managing Editor: Alysoun Owen
Editor: Jill Laidlaw

Collins
My First Book of
Transport

Contents

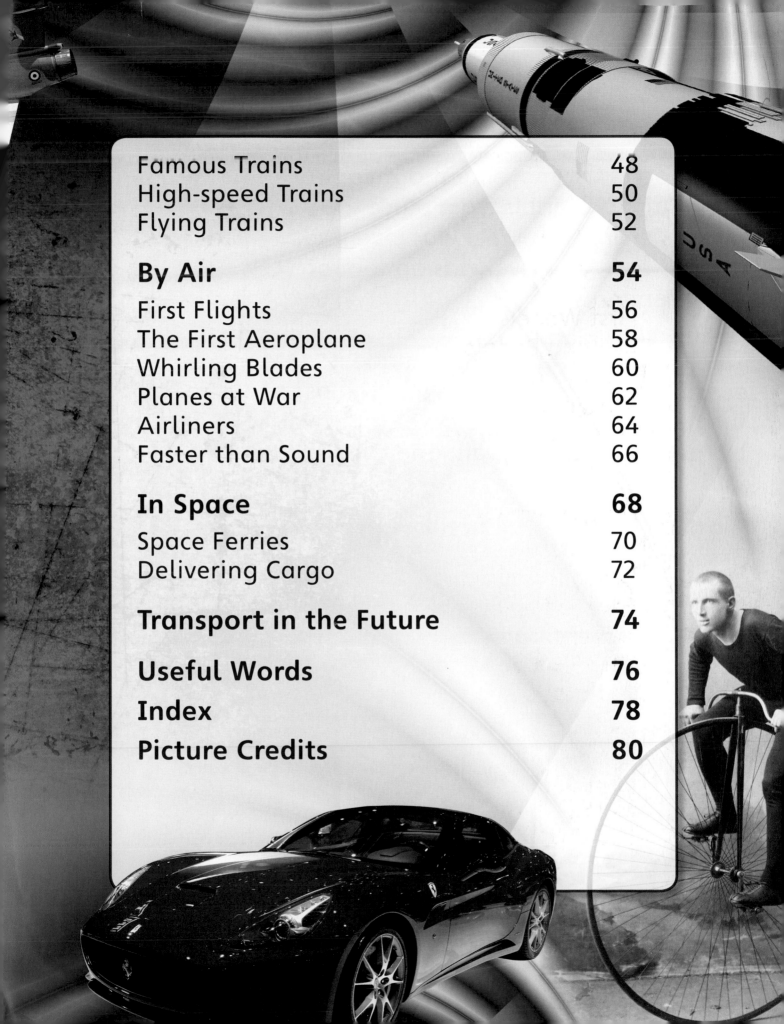

People Power

Transport is the movement of people, goods and materials from place to place. Before the wheel was invented, the only way to travel was on foot or to use animals.

The invention of the wheel made it easier to transport people and things further and faster. Today, we can travel by road, sea, air and rail, and even into space.

Long ago, the furthest anyone travelled was when they walked or drove their animals, like these sheep, to find food and shelter, or took their produce to market.

The first people had to carry their goods from place to place, and this still happens all over the world, like this man from Nepal.

Construction workers carry materials from place to place.

After the wheel was invented, animals were used to pull carts.

Transport before the Wheel

Before machines, people walked everywhere. They could only move things that were light enough to carry. Over time, people thought of ways to move heavier objects.

Dragging and carrying

A long time ago people had to move large stones or trees to build shelters. They moved these things by dragging them along the ground. They also had to move large animals they killed for food. These animals were either dragged or were hung from a pole and carried by a person at each end.

Using a pole like this lets two people share a heavy weight between them and makes it easier to carry.

Carrying seats

Rich people had servants or slaves to carry them. A rich person sat in a seat or lay in a bed that was lifted and carried along. Seats and beds that are carried like this are called litters or sedans.

Japanese emperors were carried in chairs decorated with gold.

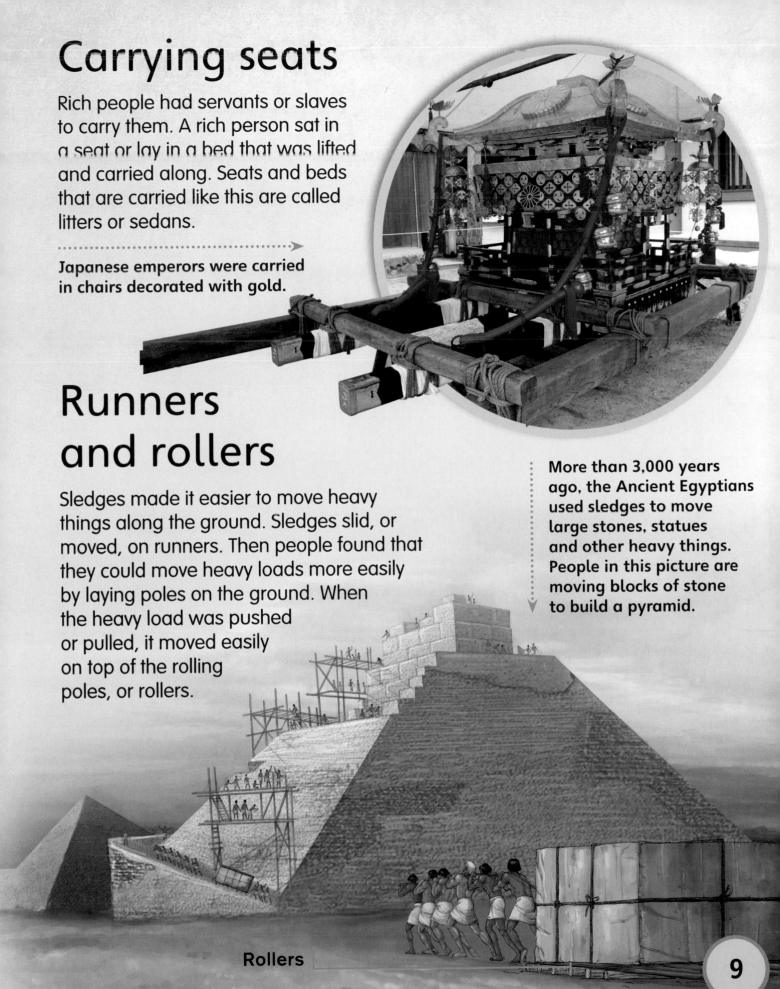

Runners and rollers

Sledges made it easier to move heavy things along the ground. Sledges slid, or moved, on runners. Then people found that they could move heavy loads more easily by laying poles on the ground. When the heavy load was pushed or pulled, it moved easily on top of the rolling poles, or rollers.

More than 3,000 years ago, the Ancient Egyptians used sledges to move large stones, statues and other heavy things. People in this picture are moving blocks of stone to build a pyramid.

Rollers

Animal Power

About 11,000 years ago, people started keeping wild animals for food, milk, fur and wool. Then they used strong animals, such as oxen, to pull heavy carts and ploughs. Other animals were trained so people could ride them.

············>
Oxen are slow, strong animals that can pull heavy carts.

Donkeys

Donkeys were some of the first animals people used for transport. They were used to carry heavy loads on their backs. Animals like this are called pack animals. Donkeys, elephants, camels, buffaloes, reindeer and llamas have all been used as pack animals.

Donkeys are easily trained to carry things, such as vegetables, sacks of grain and water.

Dog teams

One dog on its own is not very strong, but a pack of dogs working together can pull a heavy load. Dogs have been used to pull sledges for at least 4,000 years. People who live in areas near the North Pole still use dog sledges.

Dogs called huskies are the best for pulling sledges on snow. They are very strong and have a thick coat to keep them warm.

Horses

People have been riding horses for about 5,000 years. A horse can walk all day with a rider on its back or gallop at more than 40 kilometres (about 25 miles) per hour for a short time. A horse can also pull a chariot into battle or trot along pulling a cart or a carriage.

Many people like to ride horses for fun and sport. In some parts of the world, horses are also used as transport and to carry loads.

By Road

The first roads were dirt tracks made by people making the same journeys over and over again. These roads followed rivers and valleys. Today, bridges and tunnels take roads through mountains, over rivers, and even under the sea.

The Ancient Romans built great highways linking Rome, shown in this picture, to other cities of their empire. Many of these roads, built over 2,000 years ago, have been renovated and are still in use.

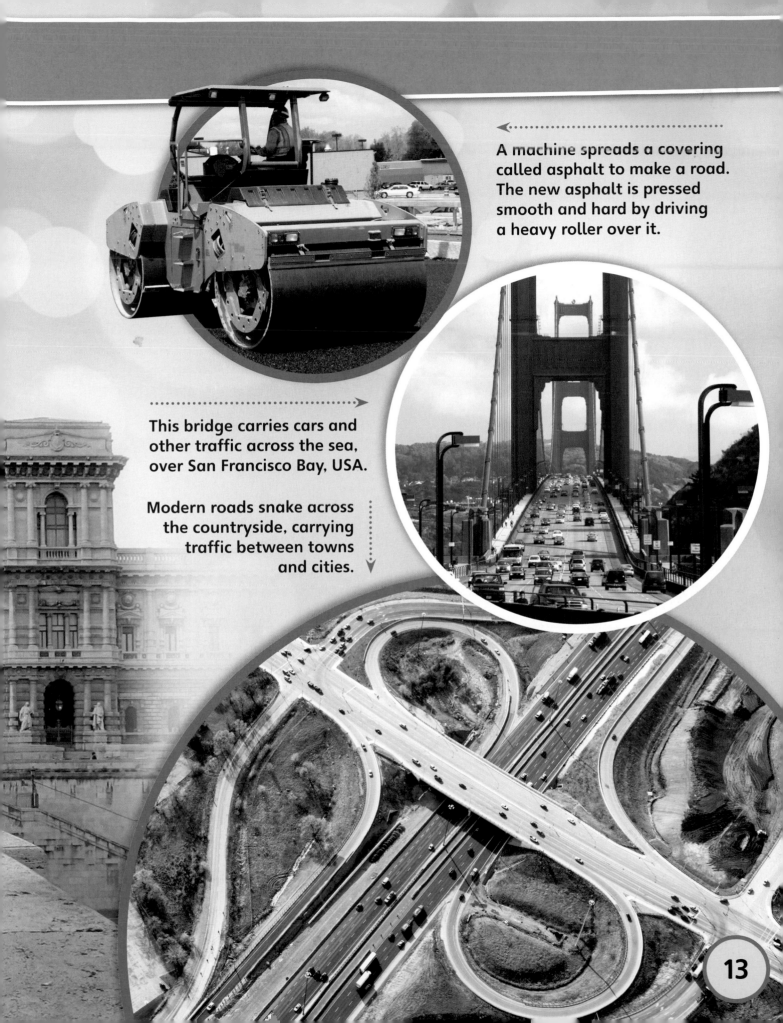

A machine spreads a covering called asphalt to make a road. The new asphalt is pressed smooth and hard by driving a heavy roller over it.

This bridge carries cars and other traffic across the sea, over San Francisco Bay, USA.

Modern roads snake across the countryside, carrying traffic between towns and cities.

First Wheels

The wheel is one of the most important inventions ever made. No-one knows who invented the wheel, because it happened so long ago. The first wheels were made about 5,500 years ago in Mesopotamia.

Wooden wheels

The first wheels were made from wooden planks joined together and then cut into a circle. A wheel made like this was stronger than a disc cut from a log or tree trunk. The first wheels were used to make farm carts.

Wheels made from planks of wood joined together were much stronger.

Wheels made from discs of wood split easily.

Wheel made from planks

Wheel made from a disc of wood

14

Tyres

To make wooden wheels last longer, a metal hoop was fitted around the outer edge. This hoop was called a tyre. Later, tyres were made of rubber and filled with air. The air made the tyres springy. Rubber tyres squash down when they run over bumps in the road and give a smoother ride. Cars, bicycles and many other vehicles now have rubber tyres.

Metal tyres were heated to make them expand, so they were easier to fit over a wooden wheel.

Saving weight

Big wheels made of thick wooden planks were very heavy. About 4,000 years ago, people found a way to make a much lighter wheel. They joined the middle of the wheel to the rim by thin rods called spokes.

Spokes made of wire make a bicycle wheel light and very strong.

Rim

Spoke

Tyre

Pushing Pedals

The bicycle is one of the most successful transport machines ever invented. There are twice as many bicycles in the world as there are cars. Bikes are used for transport and also for fun.

Funny bikes

People tried making bicycles in all sorts of different shapes and sizes before they found the best one. One of the strangest was the high-wheeler. The front wheel was huge and the back wheel was tiny. The rider sat on top of the big front wheel. High-wheelers were very hard to ride without falling off, and had no brakes.

The high-wheeler bicycle was also called the penny-farthing. It was named after two British coins—the penny and the smaller farthing.

Penny wheel

Farthing wheel

City bikes

Lots of people who live in cities ride bikes. Bikes are very good for getting through traffic quickly. It is easier to find a place to keep a bike than to find a parking place for a car, especially in busy city streets.

Some workers in big cities ride bicycles, like this tandem, to work instead of using their car or public transport.

In China, bikes are the second most common form of transport, after walking.

Pedal transport

Bikes are still the main way to travel and transport goods in some parts of the world. Bicycles can use narrow lanes and dirt tracks that are too small for cars and lorries. Also, a bicycle is often the only form of transport that many people can afford to buy.

In some places, especially in Asia and Africa, bikes are piled high with goods being taken to and from market.

Motorbikes

Motorbikes have two wheels, with an engine between the wheels. There are small motorbikes for getting through city traffic, big bikes for long journeys and sports bikes that are fun to ride.

The first motorbike

On a November day in 1885, Paul Daimler rode a new machine along a country lane in Germany. His father, Gottlieb, and Wilhelm Maybach had built it. It was the world's first motorbike. It had a top speed of 11 kilometres (about 7 miles) per hour.

A model of the first motorbike. The bike was made mostly of wood. Its wheels had wooden spokes and iron rims.

Hot seat

During the first ever motorbike ride in 1885, the engine became so hot that it set the seat on fire.

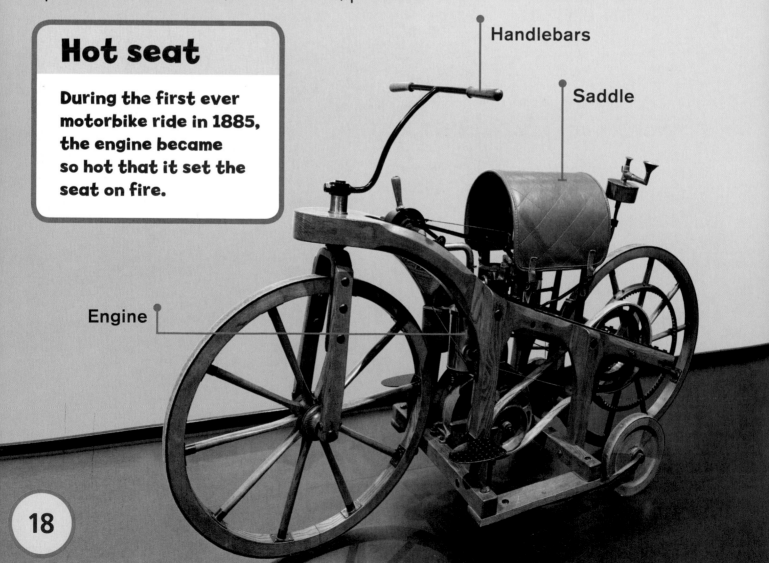

Handlebars

Saddle

Engine

Emergency!

Police forces in many countries have officers on motorbikes. Motorbikes let police officers race through traffic to reach accidents and crime scenes more quickly than a car. Some emergency health workers, called paramedics, also travel on motorbikes. This means they can reach an accident quickly, which can help save lives.

Police motorbikes are small enough to get through traffic jams and also fast enough to chase cars.

Racing bikes

There are racing bikes built for roads, racetracks and dirt tracks. Some motorbikes even race on ice! Dirt-bikes have knobbly tyres to grip the soft ground. Ice-racing bikes have tyres with metal spikes that dig into the ice so they do not slip.

The fastest racing bikes can reach a top speed of more than 320 kilometres per hour.

Motorcars

When cars were invented, they gave people more freedom to travel than ever before. At first, only wealthy people could buy cars. Soon, cars became cheaper to make and, as prices fell, more and more people could buy their own car.

Battery and steam

The very first vehicle that could move using its own power was a steam-powered tractor built in France in 1769. The first electric car was built in Scotland in the 1830s. While inventors were trying to build better steam cars and electric cars, a new fuel called petrol was being made from oil. Soon, inventors were building engines that burnt petrol.

One of the first vehicles, a steam-powered tractor, crashed into a wall in 1771. The tractor moved as fast as someone walking but was difficult to stop. ▼

Wooden wheel with metal rim

Steering wheel

Brake

Boiler to heat water to make steam

The first motorcar

Karl Benz built the first motorcar, or automobile, in Germany in 1885. It had three wheels. The front wheel turned to steer the car. It was powered by a tiny petrol engine at the back.

The first cars had a fold down hood and room for a driver and one passenger.

The Ford Model T

The Model T was the first car made in large numbers in factories. This is called mass production. More than 15 million Model Ts were built between 1908 and 1927. Mass production made the cars cheaper. This meant that many more people could buy a car.

The Ford Model T was the most important car of the 20th century. It was also known as the Tin Lizzie or Flivver.

Star car

By the time the last Model T was built in 1927, the Ford company was producing a car every 24 seconds.

Trucks and Buses

Trucks and buses are commercial vehicles, which means people pay to use them. Trucks transport goods, while buses transport people. Commercial vehicles are usually bigger and heavier than cars, so they can carry greater loads.

Types of trucks

There are many different types of trucks. Trucks that carry loose materials, such as sand, can tip up at the back to unload quickly. Articulated lorries have two parts. The front part with the driver's cab and engine is the tractor. The tractor is used to pull the second part called a semi-trailer. The tractor can quickly switch from one semi-trailer to another.

A tipper truck has a door at the back. When the container tips up, the door swings open and the load slides out.

Door swings open

Buses

People have been travelling by bus since the 1820s. The first buses were pulled by horses. Today, buses and trucks are nearly all powered by diesel engines. Buses that make longer journeys are called coaches. Coaches have more comfortable seats, more room for luggage, toilets and sometimes even video screens.

There are single-deck buses and double-deck buses.

Road trains

The longest and heaviest trucks are called road trains. They make long journeys across vast places such as Australia. The longest road trains can be more than 50 metres (about 164 feet) long and weigh more than 100 tonnes (about 98 tons). They need a very powerful tractor, called a prime mover in Australia, to pull so many trailers.

Road trains are very long trucks with two or more trailers. They can transport anything from cattle to fuel, to building materials, such as sand.

23

Modern Cars

There are many different sorts of cars. Some have lots of room inside for carrying families and their belongings. Others are small and fast, and only have room for two people. Racing cars are built to go as fast as possible to win races.

On four wheels

The most popular cars today have comfortable seats and space at the back for carrying luggage. Millions of these cars are made in factories. Sports cars are smaller cars that are fun to drive. The fastest and most powerful cars are called supercars.

One and only

The first ever race for cars was held in Paris on 28th April, 1887. A steam-powered car driven by a Frenchman, Count Jules de Dion, was declared the winner but he was the only person who entered.

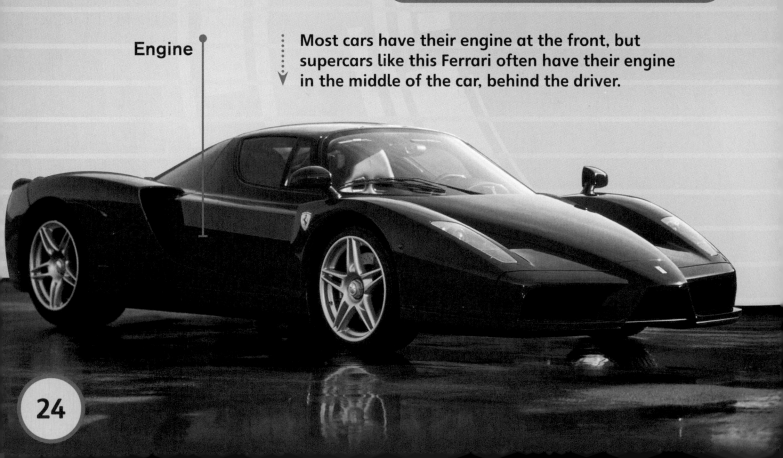

Engine

Most cars have their engine at the front, but supercars like this Ferrari often have their engine in the middle of the car, behind the driver.

Racing cars

As soon as the first cars were built, people wanted to know which one was the fastest. Special tracks were built for cars to race on. Today, some racing cars look like family cars, while others have a long, thin body with room inside for just one person.

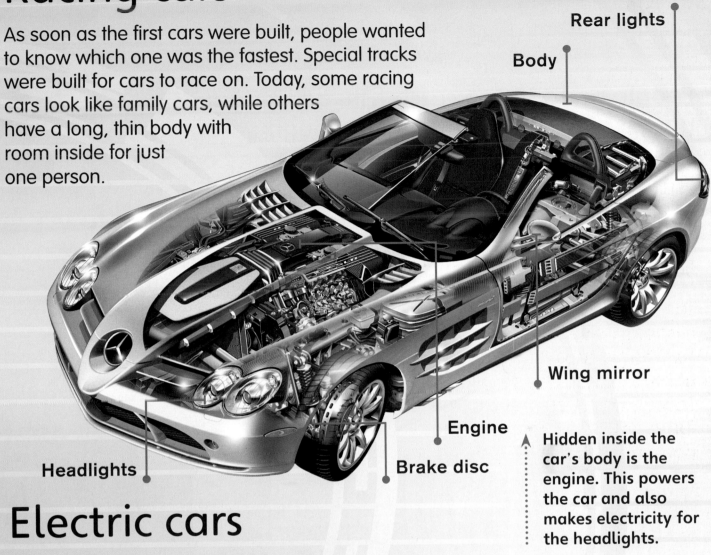

Rear lights

Body

Wing mirror

Engine

Brake disc

Headlights

Hidden inside the car's body is the engine. This powers the car and also makes electricity for the headlights.

Electric cars

Car engines work by burning fuel. When engines burn fuel, they give out nasty, smelly gases. Cars with electric motors instead of engines are cleaner and quieter. Some cars have an electric motor for short journeys in town and an engine for going faster and making longer journeys. These cars are called hybrids.

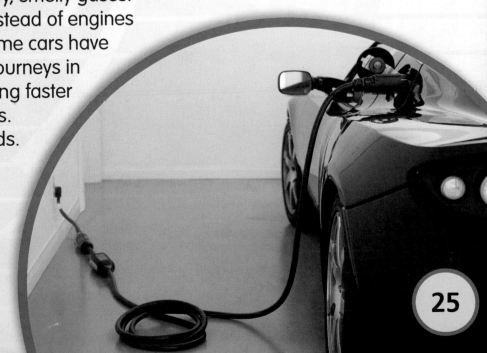

The motor in an electric car is powered by a battery. Instead of being filled up with fuel, the car is charged with electricity using an electric socket.

25

By Sea

People go to sea to catch fish, deliver goods and explore the world. Even though aeroplanes let people travel faster than ever, many people still travel by sea. Millions of people sail boats for fun and sport. Some watercraft are just big enough for one person, while others can carry thousands of people.

Ships of all sizes carry passengers and cargo between ports all over the world.

Car ferries transport motorists and their cars across water.

The fastest powerboats can cover more than 300 kilometres (about 186 miles) per hour.

Yachts use the wind in their sails to push them through the water.

The First Boats

People started travelling across water tens of thousands of years ago. They had to make their own boats from the materials they found around them. They used tree trunks, animal skins and even grass.

Boats from trees

The first people saw that fallen trees floated in rivers, so they tied tree trunks together to make rafts. They also hollowed out tree trunks to make boats called dugout canoes. They carved paddles out of wood to move the canoes through the water.

Flying maps

Viking explorer Floki Vilgerdarson released ravens to know when land was near. If a raven flew in a certain direction, the boat followed, knowing the bird was flying towards land.

The dugout canoe is one of the oldest types of boat. They are still made in some parts of the world, like Africa.

Coracles

Thousands of years ago, some people made boats by sewing animal skins over a wooden frame. The coracle is a type of skin boat. It is steered through the water by one oar. A coracle is very light, so one person can easily carry it when it is out of the water. Coracles can also be made from bamboo and covered with canvas, instead of skin.

Reed boats are still built today. They are used for fishing in countries such as Peru.

Reed boats

In some places, tall strong grasses called reeds grow by rivers and lakes. Many years ago, people cut the reeds down and tied them into bundles. Then the bundles were tied together to make a boat. Reed boats were made in Egypt 6,000 years ago.

A coracle is a small basket-shaped boat for one person. Coracles are used for transport and fishing on rivers.

An Inuit kayak is made by sewing seal skins together.

Using the Wind

For thousands of years, the only way to travel a long way in a big ship was to use the wind as a source of power. Sheets called sails were raised to catch the wind. Today, most ships have engines but people still use sail boats for fun and fishing.

Sailing ships

The oldest sailing ships had one big square sail hanging from a pole called a mast. Later, ships had more masts and more sails. Sailing ships carried cargo from place to place. Explorers sailed ships like this all over the world looking for new lands.

Large sailing ships, called tall ships, are used today for racing. They are also used to teach people how sailing ships and sailors worked in past times.

Sail

Main mast

Hull

Front or bow

Junks

A junk is a type of sailing ship that has been used in Asia for nearly 2,000 years. Small junks were sailed in rivers and in the sea near the shore. The biggest junks could cross oceans. Their sails were held open by bamboo strips.

The junk was invented in China. It is one of the oldest types of ship still sailing today.

Clipper ships

Clipper ships were the fastest of the big sailing ships. They were built in the 19th century to carry cargo that had to be transported quickly. For example, they raced each other to bring tea from China to Britain. Clippers were long and thin, so they cut through the water quickly. They also had lots of sails to catch the most wind.

The *Cutty Sark* was one of the last clipper ships. She could sail from China to Britain in about 100 days. An ordinary cargo ship could take more than a year.

Engine Power

Sailing ships could only go where the wind blew them. If there was no wind, they could not go anywhere. A ship with an engine can travel in any direction at any time.

Paddle steamers

The first engines used in boats were steam engines. Early steam ships were built more than 200 years ago. Their steam engines turned a big wheel with huge paddles. When the wheel turned, the paddles pushed the ship along.

The Mississippi River in the USA was famous for its paddle steamers. They were powered by a steam engine driving a big paddle wheel at the back of the boat.

Front of ship

Paddle wheel

Modern ships

Today, ships are no longer powered by steam engines and they do not have paddle wheels like in the past. Most modern ships are powered by diesel engines. These are like truck engines, but much bigger. The engines turn propellers that push the ship along.

Ships are built on land and then launched by sliding them into the water.

Water jets

Some ships have water jets instead of propellers. Their engines suck in seawater and shoot it out behind the ship so fast that it pushes the ship through the waves. Turning the jets to one side or the other steers the ship.

Outboard engine

Small powerboats have their engines on the outside. These are called outboard engines.

33

Warships

Warships are ships built for fighting. They are faster than other ships and have guns and other weapons on board. Some warships carry planes and helicopters with them.

Rowing to war

One of the most fearsome warships of the ancient world was the trireme, used in Ancient Greece. Triremes were rowed into battle. A ram at the front punched holes in enemy ships.

Submarines are called boats even though they are very large.

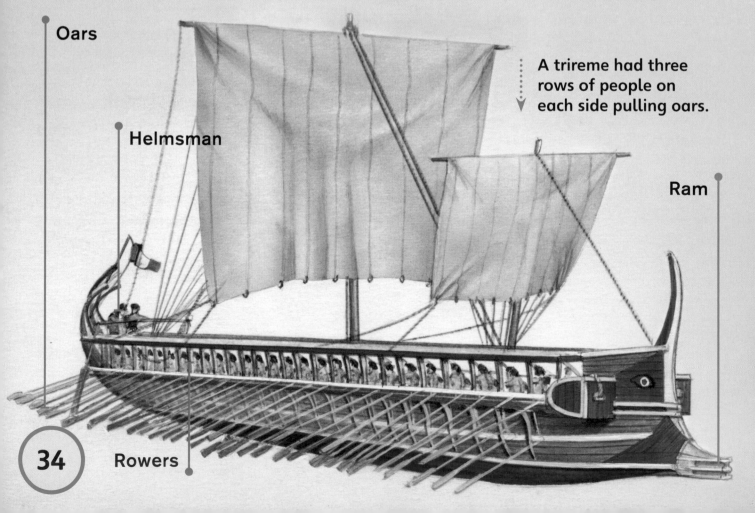

Oars

Helmsman

A trireme had three rows of people on each side pulling oars.

Ram

Rowers

Destroyers

Today, there are many different types of warships. The destroyer is the main type of warship used by modern navies. A destroyer has a crew of 200–300 sailors. Some of the crew sail the ship, while others watch out for danger and fight if an enemy attacks.

Destroyers can get to a war zone very quickly. They are armed with lots of guns and other weapons.

Aircraft carriers

Aircraft carriers are the biggest warships today. They carry planes and helicopters to war zones. The top deck of the ship is flat so the aircraft can take off and land on it. The biggest aircraft carriers are giant ships called super-carriers.

An aircraft carrier is like a floating airport. The biggest aircraft carriers have a crew of nearly 6,000 people.

Ships Today

There are lots of different types of ships. Some carry passengers and some carry passengers' cars, too. Other ships carry all sorts of loads, or cargo. Tankers are cargo ships that carry liquids, such as oil. Other cargo ships carry dry materials such as coal or wheat.

Holiday ships

Cruise ships take people on holidays at sea. They have shops, libraries and swimming pools. Passengers can also watch stage shows and films, and play sports. When cruise ships call in at ports, the passengers go ashore to see the sights.

About 15–20 million people take holidays on cruise ships every year. The largest cruise ship in the world, the *Allure of the Seas*, can carry more than 6,000 passengers. Even the slightly smaller *Brilliance of the Seas (below)* can carry more than 2,500 passengers.

Bridge

Helipad

Lifeboats

Ferry ships

Ferry ships, or ferries, are passenger ships that sail back and forth between the same ports. Some ferries carry cars, buses and trucks, as well as passengers. Giant doors in the ship open to let the vehicles drive inside. This type of ship is also called a roll-on roll-off ferry, or ro-ro.

A car ferry has a lower deck where cars and other vehicles park while the ship is at sea. The passengers stay on other decks.

Container ships

A container ship is a type of cargo ship. Container ships carry cargo packed in big metal boxes called shipping containers. The cargo inside could be almost anything, from television sets or motorbikes, to clothes or food. Each container is as big as a truck. A large container ship can carry more than 10,000 containers.

A container ship carries thousands of cargo containers piled up on the top deck, as well as inside it.

Shipping container

Racing Boats

Many different types of boats take part in races. There are races for boats with sails, and there are races for boats with engines.

Catamarans

The part of a boat that sits in the water is called the hull. Racing boats with one hull are called monohulls. Racing boats with two hulls are called catamarans. Trimarans are boats with three hulls. Catamarans and trimarans are very fast because their long, thin hulls can cut through water easily.

The biggest and fastest catamarans take part in races across oceans. Some even race around the world.

Hull

Hydroplanes are racing powerboats. They skim across the water at high speeds. Some can even cross a speed of 500 kilometres (about 311 miles) per hour.

Powerboats

Big powerboats race against each other in the sea. They stay close to the shore so that lots of people can watch the races. Some of these boats have ten times the power of a family car and they are as fast as a racing car.

America's Cup

The America's Cup is the world's oldest sailing competition. The first competition was held in 1851. The boats are built specially for the races and they are sailed by teams of the world's top sailors.

This trimaran is called *USA*. It won the America's Cup in 2010.

By Rail

Railway transport was invented in the 1800s. Railways made it possible to move more people and goods further and faster than ever before. Every day, trains carry millions of people into the towns and cities where they work.

Many millions of people use rail transport to move around their country.

The first trains were steam powered.

Diesel trains replaced steam power.

High-speed trains are electric.

Steam Pioneers

The first steam railways were made mainly to transport coal and iron. Trains just for people were designed later. The first railway engines were built by inventors and engineers such as Richard Trevithick, George Stephenson and his son, Robert Stephenson.

Birth of the railway

In 1804, Richard Trevithick invented the railway engine, or locomotive. He had already built a steam-powered carriage called *Puffing Devil* to run on roads. He built the first railway engine to pull wagons along special tracks. The engine carried iron from an iron works in Wales to a nearby canal.

Richard Trevithick's 1804 railway engine could pull 10 tonnes (9.8 tons) of iron at a speed of 8 kilometres (about 5 miles) per hour.

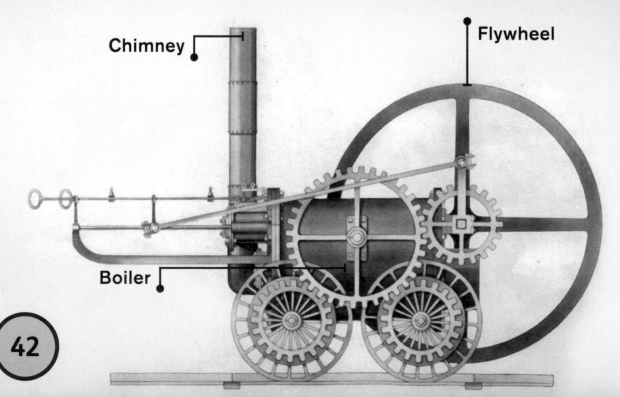

Chimney

Flywheel

Boiler

42

People trains

The world's first passenger railway opened in England in 1825. It ran between the towns of Stockton and Darlington in England, a distance of 42 kilometres (about 26 miles). The train carried both goods and people. It was pulled by an engine called *Locomotion No. 1*, built by George Stephenson. Separate goods trains and passenger trains started running in 1833.

An artist's drawing of the first railway journey by the *Locomotion No. 1* in 1825. The passengers rode in open carriages and were often covered in dirt and smoke from the engine.

Rocket

In 1829, the Liverpool and Manchester Railway Company held a competition to find the best engine to pull trains on its new railway line. The competition was called the Rainhill Trials, and 15,000 people came to watch. An engine called *Rocket* won. *Rocket* was built by George and Robert Stephenson.

Rocket had a top speed of 50 kilometres (about 31 miles) per hour, which was very fast for the 1820s.

Going Underground

It sometimes takes a long time to travel a short way across a city by car or bus because the busy streets are full of traffic. One way to go faster is to take a train that goes under the city.

Tube travel

Underground trains travel through tunnels below streets and buildings. The first underground railway was built in London. It opened in 1863. Since then, more and more tunnels have been added. Londoners call their underground railway the "Tube", because it has tube-shaped tunnels.

An underground train stops at a platform deep below the streets of London, and its doors slide open.

96447

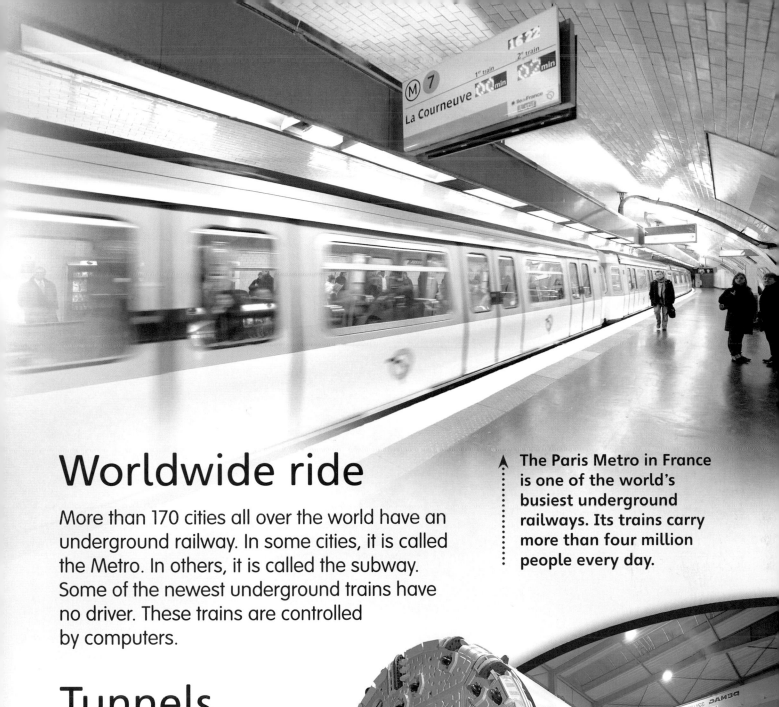

Worldwide ride

More than 170 cities all over the world have an underground railway. In some cities, it is called the Metro. In others, it is called the subway. Some of the newest underground trains have no driver. These trains are controlled by computers.

The Paris Metro in France is one of the world's busiest underground railways. Its trains carry more than four million people every day.

Tunnels

The first underground tunnels were dug by hand using picks and shovels. Today, they are dug by giant machines called tunnel-boring machines.

......................➤

A tunnel-boring machine moves through the ground like a giant worm.

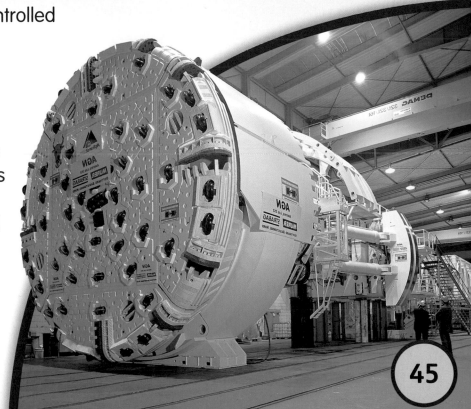

The End of Steam

Steam engines pulled trains until the 1950s. By then, a new type of railway engine was in use. It was called a diesel engine. After another ten years or so, the age of steam was over.

Diesel power

Diesel engines were easier to drive, quieter, cleaner and cheaper to run than steam engines. A steam engine took hours to get ready. Its boiler had to be filled with water and a fire had to be lit. Then the crew had to wait for the water to boil and make enough steam to start moving the engine.

......................➤
A diesel engine starts at the press of a button.

⋮
▼
A short train like this is powered by diesel motors built into the carriages.

Freight trains

Powerful diesel engines pull the heaviest and longest goods, or freight trains. It a train is too long for one diesel engine to pull, more engines can be added. In 2001, a freight train of 682 wagons and eight diesel engines ran in Australia. The train was more than 7 kilometres (about 4 miles) long and weighed about 100,000 tonnes (about 98,421 tons).

◄ ....

Transporting freight by rail takes thousands of trucks off the roads.

Steam today

Some steam trains are still running today in Britain, South Africa, Germany, Pakistan and South America. The five railways that make up the Mountain Railways of India use steam trains too. Many of these trains run on lines used by tourists.

Famous Trains

Some locomotives and trains are famous. These include the *Pioneer Zephyr, Flying Scotsman* and *Mallard*. Their names are remembered because they set speed records or had a special design.

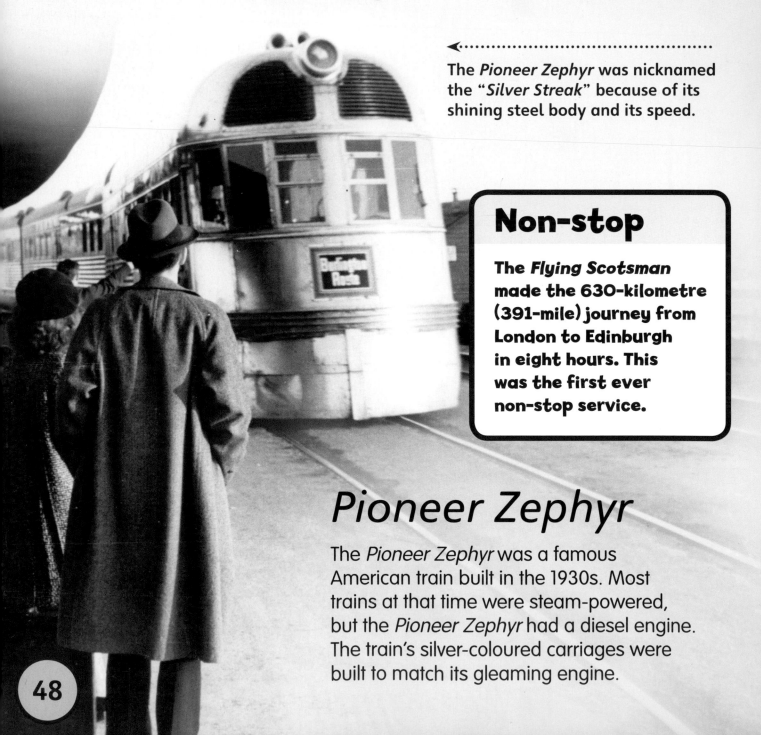

The *Pioneer Zephyr* was nicknamed the *"Silver Streak"* because of its shining steel body and its speed.

Non-stop

The *Flying Scotsman* made the 630-kilometre (391-mile) journey from London to Edinburgh in eight hours. This was the first ever non-stop service.

Pioneer Zephyr

The *Pioneer Zephyr* was a famous American train built in the 1930s. Most trains at that time were steam-powered, but the *Pioneer Zephyr* had a diesel engine. The train's silver-coloured carriages were built to match its gleaming engine.

Flying Scotsman

On 30th November 1934, a British railway engine called the *Flying Scotsman* pulled a train at a speed of 160 kilometres (about 99 miles) per hour. It was the first time that any train had gone as fast as this. The *Flying Scotsman* pulled passenger trains from the 1920s to the 1960s.

The *Flying Scotsman* was named because it pulled long-distance express trains between London and Edinburgh, in Scotland.

Mallard

A steam engine called *Mallard* set a speed record that has never been broken. On 3rd July 1938, a train pulled by *Mallard* set off from Grantham in England. During its journey to Peterborough, it reached a world record speed of 201 kilometres (about 125 miles) per hour. This record may never be broken because steam express trains are not built any more.

Mallard's special shape helped it to go faster than any other steam engine.

High-speed Trains

High-speed trains are the world's fastest passenger trains. They are so fast and comfortable that many travellers choose to make long journeys by train instead of by aeroplane.

Bullet trains

Japan was the first country to build high-speed trains. Its trains were nicknamed "bullet trains", because of their shape and speed. The first bullet trains in 1963 had a top speed of 210 kilometres (about 130 miles) per hour. Bullet trains are even faster today.

Passengers have made nearly seven billion journeys in Japan's bullet trains since the 1960s.

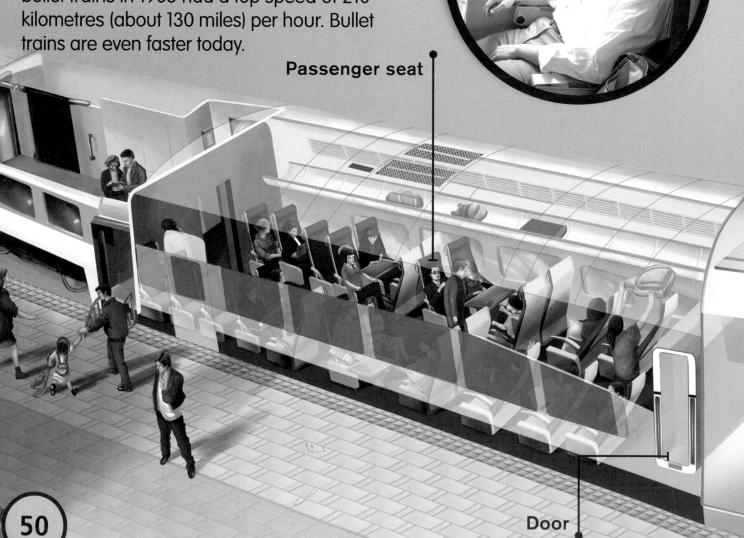

Passenger seat

Door

Going faster

High-speed trains are powered by electricity. Their wheels are turned by electric motors. Electricity for the motors comes from wires hanging above the track. The track has no tight bends, because tight bends would slow the trains down.

The German ICE (Inter-city Express) is one of the fastest passenger trains in the world.

Record-breakers

High-speed trains have set lots of speed records. The fastest of all passenger trains is a French train called TGV. On 3rd April 2007, a TGV train reached a speed of 574 kilometres (about 357 miles) per hour.

TGV trains carry passengers at up to 320 kilometres (about 199 miles) per hour. These high-speed trains are as powerful as 60 family cars.

Wheels

Controls

Driver

Flying Trains

The fastest trains have no wheels. They fly above their track! These amazing trains are called maglevs. They fly, but they don't have wings or jet engines. They use magnets to rise into the air.

Magnetic trains

If you put two magnets close to each other, they snap together or fly apart. The magnets inside a maglev train and its special track are so strong that they can lift the whole train. Magnets also make the train travel along the track. Maglevs can go faster than other trains because they don't touch their track. They glide silently above it. Maglevs get their name from magnetic levitation, since magnets help them to levitate, or rise.

This maglev is called *Transrapid*. It was built in Germany. It glides along a special track called a guideway.

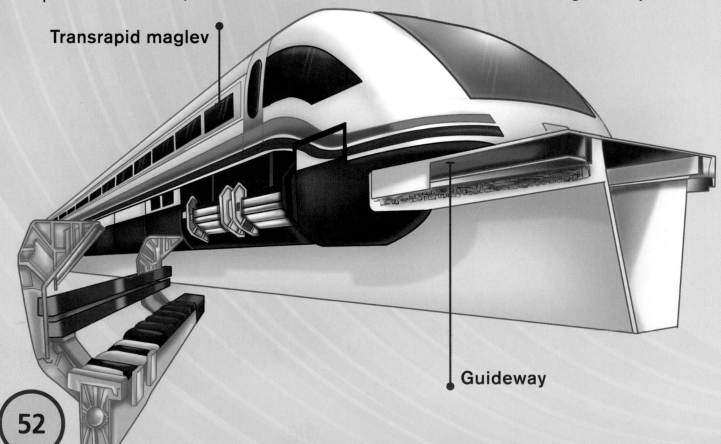

Transrapid maglev

Guideway

Carrying passengers

Maglev trains first started carrying passengers in China in 2004. These trains carry people between Shanghai and its nearby airport. The trains whiz along as fast as 430 kilometres (about 267 miles) per hour.

Travellers in Shanghai, China, can ride a super-fast maglev train. It covers the 30-kilometre (19-mile) route in just under eight minutes.

Record breaker

The world's fastest train is a maglev called MLX01. It was built in Japan for scientists and engineers to test. It does not carry paying passengers. When being tested in 2003, it went faster than any train had ever gone before. It reached a speed of 581 kilometres (about 361 miles) per hour.

The Japanese maglev train, MLX01, speeds along its test track. It flies along,10 centimetres (about 4 inches) above its track.

53

By Air

It is hard to think of our world without air travel. Every day, thousands of aeroplanes take off and fly passengers and cargo around the world. Many smaller planes and helicopters buzz around the sky too. The fastest aircraft can fly faster than the speed of sound.

An aeroplane takes off at the beginning of a journey across the world.

Many people like to fly their own aircraft. For this, they use small, light aircraft.

Jet fighters are military planes that fight battles in the sky.

Helicopters can hover in one spot.

First Flights

People flew for the first time in 1783. They were lifted off the ground by a hot-air balloon. The flights lasted just a few minutes, but they showed that it was possible for people to fly.

Making balloons

People had made toy balloons for centuries. Then two brothers in France, Joseph-Michel and Jacques-Étienne Montgolfier, wondered if a very big balloon could lift a person into the air. They built balloons made of cloth and paper. A fire under the balloon heated the air inside it. Hot air is lighter than cold air and so it lifted the balloon off the ground.

When the first hot-air balloons flew, it looked like magic.

The first flyers

On 19th September 1783, the Montgolfier brothers launched a test balloon carrying passengers for the first time. The lucky travellers were not people, they were a sheep, a duck and a rooster. All the animals landed safely.

The first balloon to carry people reached a height of more than 900 metres (about 2,953 feet) above the ground.

Up and away

On 21st November 1783, the Montgolfier brothers decided to try human passengers in their next balloon. Two people made a 25-minute flight over Paris and were the first people ever to fly.

Airships

Balloons go where the wind blows them. In 1852, Henri Giffard hung a steam engine under a balloon. This turned a propeller so the balloon, or airship, could be steered in any direction.

Frenchman Henri Giffard made the first airship flight over Paris on 24th September 1852.

e First Aeroplane

In 1903, two American brothers made history. They did something that no-one had ever done before. They built the first ever aeroplane and flew it.

The Wright brothers

Before they made planes, Wilbur and Orville Wright made kites and gliders. They went to the seaside, where it was windy, to fly them. Gliders are aeroplanes with no engines. Once they knew how to fly gliders, they wanted to build a plane with an engine that would stay in the air longer than a glider.

Orville Wright (left) and his brother Wilbur spent their lives inventing new machines.

In 1902, the Wright brothers tested their gliders over the sandy slopes of Kitty Hawk in North Carolina.

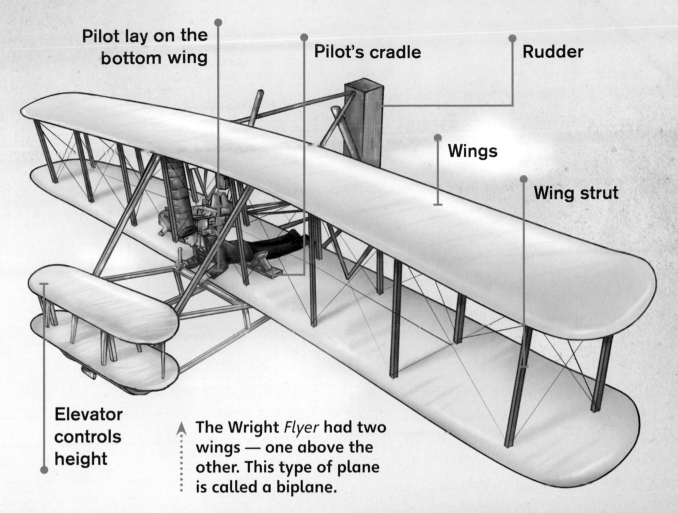

Pilot lay on the bottom wing

Pilot's cradle

Rudder

Wings

Wing strut

Elevator controls height

The Wright *Flyer* had two wings — one above the other. This type of plane is called a biplane.

Making history

The brothers, Wilbur and Orville Wright, built a plane called *Flyer*. It was made from fabric stretched over a wooden frame. Then they made their own engine and propellers for it. On 14th December 1903, Wilbur tried to fly it, but it crashed. Three days later, Orville tried. This time, the plane rose into the air and flew.

Taking off

On 17th December 1903, Orville Wright took the *Flyer* on a flight that lasted for 12 seconds. This was the first powered flight with a human pilot in history.

Orville Wright made the first ever flight of a plane with an engine. He was watched by his brother Wilbur.

Whirling Blades

Helicopters are aircraft that fly in ways that aeroplanes cannot fly. They can take off straight up and they can even stop mid-air and hover. They are able to fly in these amazing ways because of their whirling blades.

Parts of a helicopter

A helicopter has a set of long thin wings, called rotor blades, on top. When they spin very fast, they lift the helicopter up into the air. A set of smaller rotor blades at the end of the tail stops the whole helicopter from spinning.

The rotor blades on top of a helicopter may be as long as 10 metres (about 33 feet), but only a few centimetres wide.

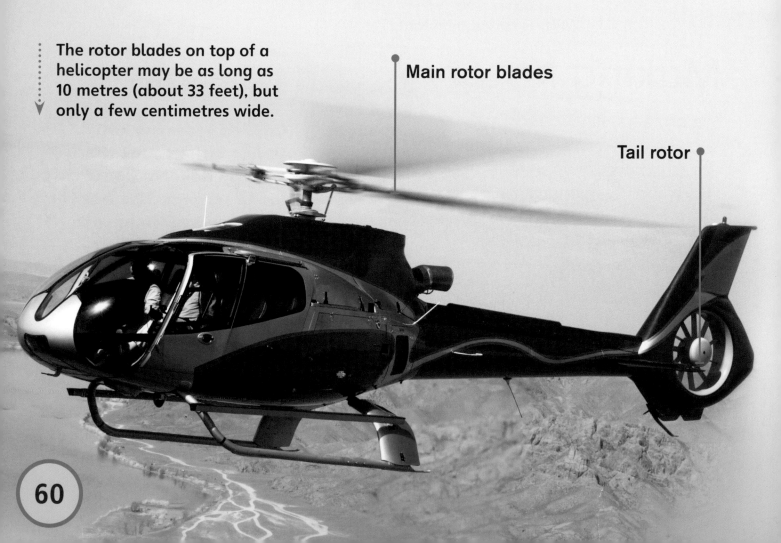

Main rotor blades

Tail rotor

Helicopters at work

Helicopters are used to rescue people in trouble because they can reach difficult places such as a mountaintop or cliff. Some work as air ambulances and can take people to hospital faster than an ambulance on a road. Helicopters are also used by the police to watch cars and people on the ground.

Helicopters at war

Armies and air forces use small helicopters to carry out attacks with guns and rockets. Bigger helicopters move soldiers and equipment from place to place. Transport helicopters can fly faster than trucks travelling by road and they are harder for an enemy to attack.

A helicopter is used to rescue someone in trouble at sea.

The Chinook is a transport helicopter. It has two sets of rotor blades on top, one set at each end.

61

Planes at War

At first, no one knew what to do with aeroplanes in a war, so they were used to watch what enemy forces were doing. Soon, planes were carrying guns to shoot at other aircraft and to drop bombs on the ground. Today, different types of warplanes do a wide range of jobs.

Fighters

Fighters are small, fast planes that attack other aircraft. Some fighters can also drop bombs. The fastest fighters can fly at more than 2,000 kilometres (about 1,243 miles) per hour, or nearly three times faster than an airliner.

The F-22 is an American fighter. Its pilot sits in front of the plane's two powerful jet engines.

The C-17 Globemaster is a transport plane. It can carry more than 77 tonnes (about 76 tons) of cargo.

Bombers

Bombers are planes that drop bombs on the ground. They are bigger and slower than fighters. In the past, large bombers were used in great numbers, such as the Lancaster bomber in the Second World War. There are very few bomber aircraft in use today because big, slow bombers are easy to shoot down.

▲ The B-2 Spirit is a bomber. Its strange shape is called a flying wing.

Transporters

Lots of soldiers, heavy equipment and supplies often have to be moved a long way very quickly during a war. This is the job of transport planes. They have a big body that can carry many passengers, or lots of cargo. The back of the plane opens so that trucks can be driven straight inside.

Airliners

An airliner is a large aeroplane that carries passengers who have paid to travel. Air travel was so expensive until the 1960s that only rich people could travel by an airliner. Today, air travel is much cheaper, so millions of people take flights every year.

Jet engines

All but the smallest airliners have jet engines. A jet engine sucks air in at the front and heats it up by burning fuel. When the air heats up, it expands and rushes out through the back of the engine. The jets from an airliner's engines push the aeroplane through the air.

An airliner's jet engine is called a turbofan. It is like a big heater. It heats up air so fast that it flies out of the engine and pushes the plane forwards.

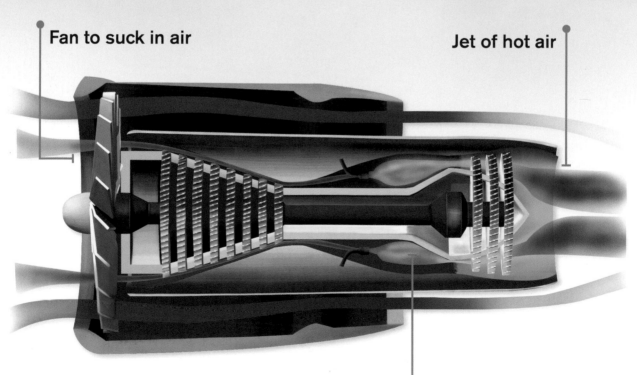

Fan to suck in air

Jet of hot air

Fuel burned here

Short flights

Small airliners with two engines fly passengers on journeys taking up to about three hours. These journeys are called short-haul flights. Most of these aeroplanes carry about 100–200 passengers.

More Boeing 737 airliners have been built than any other airliner. Nearly 7,000 of them have been produced since the 1960s.

Long flights

The biggest airliners with four jet engines make the longest flights. These flights take more than six hours. Flights as long as this are called long-haul flights. Most long-flight airliners carry 250-450 passengers.

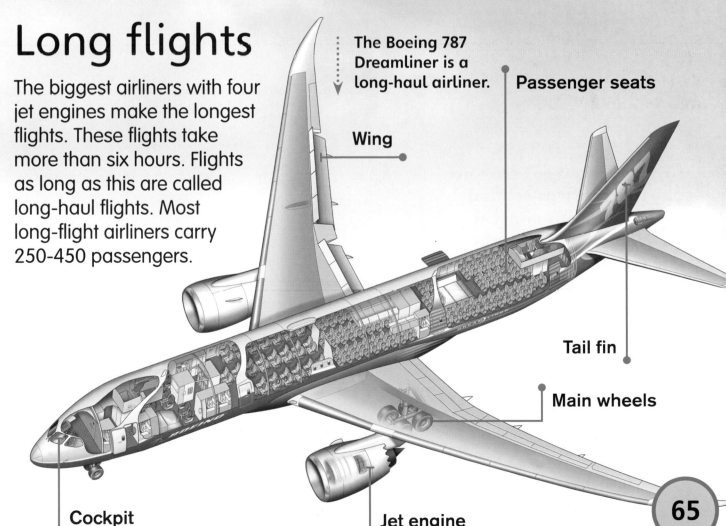

The Boeing 787 Dreamliner is a long-haul airliner.

Passenger seats

Wing

Tail fin

Main wheels

Cockpit

Jet engine

Faster than Sound

When aeroplanes flew as fast as they could in the 1940s, something strange happened. They shook about so much that some of them even crashed. They were flying nearly as fast as sound, but they could not go any faster.

Rocket plane

A plane called the X-1 was built to try to fly faster than sound. It had a rocket in its tail to help it to go as fast as possible. Its pointy nose helped it, too. It worked. The X-1 was the first aeroplane to fly faster than sound.

Super-plane

The X-1 could not take off by itself. It was carried up into the air under a B-29 bomber. When the bomber dropped the X-1, the pilot fired its rocket and it soared away.

The X-1 rocket-plane was the first supersonic plane. Supersonic means faster than sound.

Fast fighters

Today, nearly all fighter planes can fly faster than sound. Some fighters can fly twice as fast as sound. Their speed helps them to catch up with other aircraft. It also helps them to fly away from danger.

The Eurofighter Typhoon is one of the world's fastest fighters. It can fly at twice the speed of sound.

Concorde

In November 1961, Britain and France got together to build a supersonic passenger aircraft called Concorde. It looked a bit like a paper dart. Concorde carried about 100 people at 2,125 kilometres (about 1,320 miles) per hour, or about twice the speed of sound. It made its first flight in 1969. After seven years of testing, it started carrying passengers in 1976. It continued flying until 2003.

Concorde carried passengers more than twice as fast as other airliners.

In Space

Space transport is the newest kind of transport. When the USA and Russia wanted to send people into space in the 1960s, they had to build spacecraft to transport them. The first manned spacecraft were tiny. The American *Mercury* and Russian *Vostok* craft were just big enough for one person to squeeze inside.

A giant *Saturn V* rocket blasts off with an *Apollo* spacecraft on top.

The *Apollo* spacecraft carried astronauts to the moon.

An *Apollo* spacecraft was changed so that it could link up with a Russian *Soyuz* spacecraft in 1975.

A *Progress* cargo craft docks with the International Space Station beside a *Soyuz* spacecraft.

Space Ferries

Astronauts who live and work in a space station travel between Earth and space by spacecraft. Three types of spacecraft have been used as space ferries — *Apollo*, *Soyuz* and the *Space Shuttle*.

Space Shuttle

The *Space Shuttle* was the first spacecraft that could be used over and over again. It took astronauts to two space stations—the Russian Mir space station and the International Space Station.

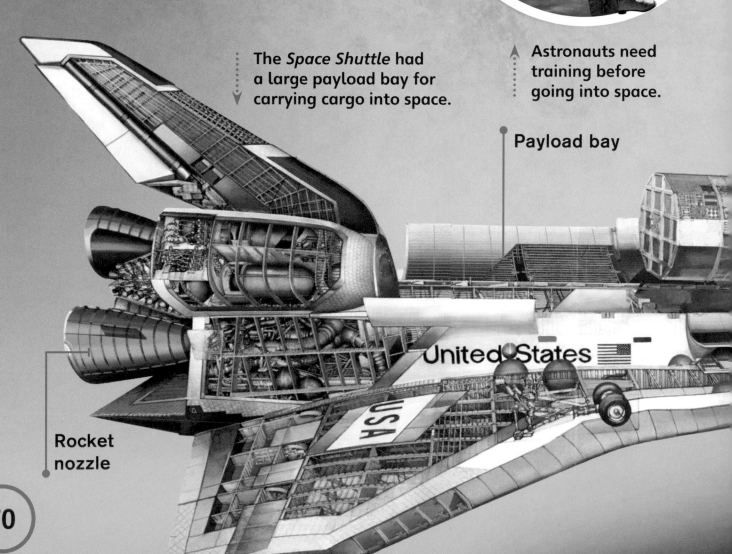

The *Space Shuttle* had a large payload bay for carrying cargo into space.

Astronauts need training before going into space.

Payload bay

United States

USA

Rocket nozzle

Apollo

The first American space station was called Skylab. It was in space from 1973 to 1979. Astronauts travelled to and from Skylab in an *Apollo* spacecraft. The *Apollo* spacecraft was built to take astronauts to the Moon. Skylab astronauts used spare spacecraft left over from the Moon flights.

The *Apollo* spacecraft had room inside for three astronauts.

Soyuz

Russian *Soyuz* spacecraft have carried astronauts to eight space stations. These included six of the seven Russian Salyut space stations, the Russian Mir space station and the International Space Station. The International Space Station is a giant spacecraft being built in space by 16 countries.

A *Soyuz* spacecraft can carry three astronauts. *Soyuz* spacecraft have been transporting astronauts since 1967.

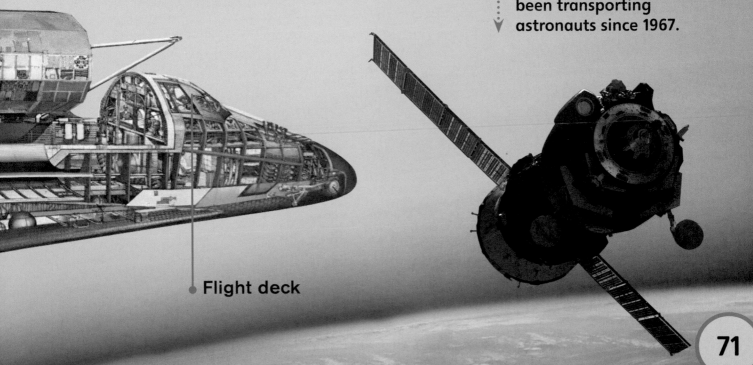

Flight deck

Delivering Cargo

Food, water and rocket fuel have to be transported from Earth to the International Space Station. These supplies are delivered by spacecraft. The craft carrying cargo have no people inside. Computers steer them towards the space station.

Space truck

Three or four times a year, Russian spacecraft called *Progress* take supplies to the International Space Station. When a *Progress* craft arrives, it locks itself onto a special door, called a docking port, on the space station. Then the astronauts inside the space station open the door and unload the supplies.

A *Progress* cargo craft docks with the International Space Station to unload its cargo.

A Russian *Progress* cargo spacecraft flies towards the International Space Station.

Jumbo cargo craft

The Automated Transfer Vehicle, or ATV, is another type of cargo spacecraft. The ATV is newer and bigger than a *Progress* spacecraft. ATVs are built in Europe. An ATV delivers more than 7 tonnes (about 6.8 tons) of cargo to the International Space Station. The first ATV was launched in 2008.

An ATV cargo craft prepares to deliver supplies to the International Space Station.

Trash collector

The *Jules Verne* delivered fuel, oxygen, food and water to the International Space Station. It was later filled with space junk and sent to burn up over the South Pacific, on its way back to Earth.

Space waste

Space station astronauts cannot throw their rubbish out into space, because it might hit a spacecraft. The rubbish is loaded into an empty cargo spacecraft. Then the spacecraft is sent down to Earth. As it dives towards the ground it gets so hot that it burns up.

An ATV cargo spacecraft is sealed inside a rocket's nose cone and prepared for launch.

Transport in the Future

Inventors are still thinking of new ways for people to travel and to transport goods. No one knows what ideas will be successful or popular in the future. Maybe we will travel in flying cars or take trips into space, like astronauts.

Flying into space

In 2004, a rocket-plane called *SpaceShipOne* flew into space and came back to Earth. It was the first manned spacecraft that was not the work of a government or space agency. It was built and flown by a private company. The same company is building bigger space planes to carry passengers into space. Soon, regular people may be able to make trips into space, not just astronauts.

Pilot Mike Melvill stands on the *SpaceShipOne* rocket-plane that he has just flown into space for the first time.

Eco-friendly cars

Most cars have engines that burn fuel made from oil that was formed deep underground millions of years ago. This oil is bad for the environment. So people are trying to find new fuels, like vegetable oil, to run their cars in the future.

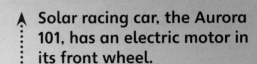

Further in the future

Who knows what sorts of vehicles we might be using for travel in just a few years. Giant cargo airships could be gliding through the sky. Rocket-powered airliners could be crossing the oceans in a fraction of the time it takes today. What do you think?

Solar racing car, the Aurora 101, has an electric motor in its front wheel.

..............................➤

The monocycle looks like a very strange way to travel. Will it be a success or a failure? Will we see lots of monocycles on our streets or will it just disappear?

Useful Words

aeroplane A powered aircraft with wings.

airliner A large aircraft that carries paying passengers.

airport A place where military, passenger and cargo planes take off and land.

airship An aircraft that flies because it is full of a gas that is lighter than air. Unlike balloons, airships can be steered.

ambulance A vehicle that takes people to hospital quickly.

astronaut A person who travels into space. Russian astronauts are also called cosmonauts.

balloon An aircraft that flies because it is full of a very light gas, such as hot air or helium.

boat A craft or vessel for travelling on or in water.

cargo Goods or materials carried by a ship, truck, spacecraft, aircraft or train.

carriages Section of a train or horse-drawn vehicle that carries passengers.

cart An open wagon or vehicle for carrying things, that is pushed or pulled by people or animals.

catamaran A boat or ship with two hulls, one beside the other.

chariot A light, two-wheel or four-wheel carriage pulled by one or more horses.

commercial vehicles Vehicles such as buses and trucks that transport passengers, goods or materials for payment.

engine A machine that burns fuel to produce power or movement.

engineer A person who uses mathematics and science to solve practical problems.

explorers People who travel the world looking for new places, people or information.

express train A train that makes long journeys without stopping at many stations on the way so that it can keep going at high speed.

freight Another word for cargo.

fuel A material such as coal or petrol that is burned to make an engine work.

glider An aeroplane that has no engine. Gliders are also called sailplanes.

helicopter An aircraft that flies by using a set of spinning blades.

jet engine An engine that makes a fast jet of air to push a plane along.

locomotive A railway engine; an engine that pulls a train.

lorries Another word for trucks.

maglev A magnetic levitation train, a train that uses the power of magnets to fly above its special track, or guideway.

mast A pole that is fixed into a boat or ship for holding up sails.

monocycle A vehicle with one wheel.

oar A pole with a flat blade at one end for moving a boat through water.

pack animals Animals used for transporting heavy things on their back.

passenger A person who travels in a bus, car, ship, train, spacecraft or aircraft but does not drive or operate the vehicle.

pilot Someone who flies an aircraft.

propellers Parts of boats, ships or aeroplanes with blades that spin and move the vehicle through the water or air.

railways The trains that carry people and goods, and the tracks on which they run.

ram A long, strong pointed piece of wood — usually a whole tree trunk — used to batter down doors or puncture holes in the sides of ships at sea.

rocket-plane A rocket-powered aircraft with wings.

rockets Space vehicles powered by rocket motors.

ship A large sea-going craft that carries passengers or cargo, or both.

sledge A vehicle that moves by sliding along the ground. Also called a sled or a sleigh.

space station A large spacecraft that stays in space for a long time with astronauts living and working inside it.

spacecraft A vehicle or craft designed to travel in space.

submarine A large water-craft that can travel deep under the water for a long time.

subway A railway that goes underground.

supersonic Faster than the speed of sound.

tourists People who travel for pleasure, because they want to see different places.

transport The movement of people, goods and materials from place to place.

trimaran A boat or ship with three hulls side by side.

trireme An Ancient Greek warship with three rows of oars on each side.

vehicle A car, train, plane or other transport machine.

wagon A railway cart for carrying freight, pulled by an engine.

Index

Picture Credits

t=top; b=bottom; bl= bottom left; br=bottom right; bc=bottom centre; tl=top left
tr=top right; tc=top centre; c=centre; tcl=top centre left; tcr=top centre right;
bcl=bottom centre left; bcr=bottom centre right

Cover: © Shutterstock.com: Andrey Yurlov

Title: © Shutterstock.com: Andrey Yurlov

Half Title: © Shutterstock.com: Andrey Yurlov

Content Page: Bigstock: Paul Campbel, Neale Cousland, Jaak Kadak, Maksim Toome, Kovalenko Iurii;
Library of Congress: Eisenmann, N.Y

Inside:

123RF: Sam D'cruz P9(t); Robert Asento P13(t); **Adrian Pingstone:** P67(t); **Bigstock:** Lucian Coman
P11(b); VibrantImage P23(t), P78; Neale Cousland P23(b); Manfred Steinbach P27(t); Andres P31(b); Lars
Christensen P37(t); Dusko matic P40-41; Jeff P41(b); Jyothi Joshi P44; Philip Lange P51(t), P77(b); **BMW
ORACLE:** Gilles Martin-Raget P27(b), P39(b); Herrenknecht AG P45(b); **Boeing:** P62-63; **Cilac Patrimoine
Industriel:** P20; **Dreamstime:** Wxin P53(t); **ESA:** S. Corvaja P73(b); **Fotolia:** Eugene O. P14; Gaelj P29(c);
Dzain P30; Stephane Henrard P31(t); Wahn P32; Crimson P38; **Ferrari:** P24; **Getty Images:** David McLain/
Aurora P11(t); Topical Press Agency/Hulton Archive P15(t); Mirco Lazzari/Getty Images Sport P19(b); Dorling
Kindersley/The Agency Collection P34(b); Panoramic Images P41(b); Koichi Kamoshida/Getty Images News
P53(b); Robert Laberge/Getty Images News P74-75; **iStockphoto:** Kali Nine LLC P7(c); Prill Mediendesign
& Fotografie P12-13; Jim Jurica P13(c); Stacey Newman P13(b); Sumbul P22; Grzegorz Malec P33(b); Rusm
P36; David Partington P46(b); **Idea Marketing:** Vittorio Ubertone P27(c); Vittorio Ubertone P39(t); **Library
of Congress:** Library of Congress Prints and Photographs Division Washington, D.C P7(b); Eisenmann,
N.Y. P16; Harris & Ewing P21(t); Vachon John P48; A.G. Renstrom/ Tissandier Collection P57(t); Tissandier
Collection P56; Daniels, John T P58-59; Wright Brothers Negatives P58(b); **Lockheed Martin Aeronautics
Company:** P55(c), P62(b); **Masterfile:** Transtock P19(t); Robert Harding P29(t); Janet Foster P29(b); R. Ian
Lloyd P47(t); **Mary Evans Picture Library:** Edwin Mullan Collection P43(t); Mercedes-Benz Cars P21(t); **NASA:**
Robert A. Hoover P66(b); P68-69; Stennis Space Centre P69(t), P69(c), P69(b); NASA, ISS Expedition 11
Crew P70-71; P70(t), P71(t), P72(t), P72(b), P73(t); **National Air and Space Museum:** Smithsonian Institution
P57(b); **Photolibrary:** Axel Schmies P18; Michael Weber P45(t); National Geographic Society P46(t); Claver
Carroll P49(t); Gordon Nicholson P49(b); Eye Ubiquitous P50(t); Eye Ubiquitous P66-67(b); Glenn Paulina
P75(b); **Shutterstock:** Zzvet P7(t); Gelia P10(b); Jiri Haureljuk P28; Jeffery Stone P37(b); Meoita P43(b); Pablo
Scapinachis P54-55; Ivan Cholakov Gostock-dot-net P64-65(t); **Superstock:** Francois Jacquemin P17(c);
Science Museum, London: The British Railway Locomotive P42; **Tesla:** P25(b); **Thinkstock:** iStockphoto
P6-7, P55(t), P55(b), P60, P76-77(t); Brand X Pictures P10(t); Jupiterimages/liquidlibrary P15(b); Ryan McVay/
Photodisc P17(t); Medioimages/Photodisc P17(b), P76(b); Hemera P26-27, P41(t), P47(b); **The United States
Navy:** Jennifer L. Walker P34(t); Northop Grumman P35(t); James Thierry P35(b); Tiger Martinez P61(t); **U.S.
Department of Defense:** Walter Reeves P61(b); **United States Air Force:** P58(c), P63(t); **United States Coast
Guard:** P33(t); **Q2AMedia Art Bank:** P8; P9(b); P50-51(b); P52; P59(t); P64.